Scratch

Scratch
Charlotte Corbeil-Coleman

Playwrights Canada Press
Toronto • Canada

PLAYWRIGHTS CANADA PRESS
The Canadian Drama Publisher
215 Spadina Ave., Suite 230, Toronto, Ontario Canada M5T 2C7
phone 416.703.0013   fax 416.408.3402
orders@playwrightscanada.com • www.playwrightscanada.com

For amateur or professional production rights, please contact
Celia Chassels of the Gary Goddard Agency
10 St. Mary Street, #305
Toronto, ON M4Y 1P9
phone: 416-928-0299, fax: 416-924-9593, email: celiachasselsgga@bellnet.ca

The publisher acknowledges the support of the Canadian taxpayers through the Government of Canada Book Publishing Industry Development Program, the Canada Council for the Arts, the Ontario Arts Council, and the Ontario Media Development Corporation.

Cover painting by Iris Turcott
Cover and type design design by Blake Sproule

LIBRARY AND ARCHIVES CANADA CATALOGUING IN PUBLICATION

Corbeil-Coleman, Charlotte
Scratch / Charlotte Corbeil-Coleman.

A play.
ISBN 978-0-88754-912-0

I. Title.

PS8555.O595S37 2010   C812'.6   C2009-907509-1

First edition: February 2010
Printed and bound by Canadian Printco, Scarborough

This play is dedicated to Mary Ann and Molly

Scratch was first workshopped by the Canadian Stage Company's RAW RAW RAW Festival of new work in 2006. It was nominated for Outstanding New Play award at the 2009 Dora Awards and won the Herman Voaden National Playwriting Award, receiving a workshop through the Thousand Island Playhouse and the Queens Drama Department. It was first produced at Factory Theatre in October of 2008.

Original Cast:

Madelyn	Monica Dotter
Anna	Charlotte Corbeil-Coleman
Mother	Marry Ann McDonald
Father	Kevin Bundy
Aunt	Catherine Fitch
Poet	Ryan Hollyman

Direced by ahdri zhina mandiela
Set and costume design by Kelly Wolf
Lighting design by Rebecca Picherack
Sound design by Steve Marsh
Assistant direction by Joan M. Kivanda
Dramaturgy by Iris Turcott

The playwright acknowledges the assistance of the 2008 Banff Playwrights Colony—a partnership between the Canada Council for the Arts, the Banff Centre, and the Alberta Arts Project.

Cast of Characters

ANNA   A young girl with lice
MADELYN   Anna's best friend
MOTHER   Anna's mother
FATHER   Anna's father
AUNT   Anna's aunt
POET   A young man who prepares food for Mother

Aunt and Poet can play all other characters

Note

All the characters tell the story together, they all move through time and space. The play should be performed in a very physical way. All characters should remain on stage until the very end. Anna's hair should be wild, dramatic, and chaotic. Itching should be used as a device to create and heighten tension.

The punctuation in this play is to be used as a tool for the actor to describe the rhythm of speaking. Em dashes at the end of a sentence indicate a cutting off or interruption of thought, either by the character who is speaking or by the next character to speak. Ellipses indicate a slight pause and a search for words. Lines ending without a period indicate a continuation of rhythm for the next character to speak.

Lights up on a girl alone on stage, she is scratching her head furiously.

ANNA   My mother is dying... and I have lice.... Fuck.

MADELYN   If I were to tell you this story, I would teach you how to stay very still and watch; I would teach you how to fall in love with something that doesn't belong to you, like a colour. I would show you how to fall in love with yellow.

POET   If it were my story, I would tell it through the doors in my house as a child. The way my parents closed doors at each other, like their mouths: they'd snap 'em shut. Slam. Slam. Slam. I lived in a house that spoke only doors for seventeen years. If this were my story, I'd tell you how I met her, how we danced up our pain all pretty.

AUNT   If this were my story, I would tell of my week. Of my husband who plays poker on Tuesdays and vacuums on Saturdays. Of my house that has candles and angel statues and fresh Kleenex, always. Of my two daughters who have matching tattoos of half moons on their hips. Who call every Thursday at seven thirty-five, both moved to the West Coast to find themselves. Both found themselves as far away from me as possible. If this were my story you would know what it was like to be kept out.

FATHER	If this were my story, I would tell the story of being born three times. The first in a farmhouse that rocked; cradled by a fierce wind, in the dry prairies. The second in Jamaica, nestled in the sand, in the sun, and in the sky. Being high, smoking the sweetest of sweets and listening to reggae like it was my mother's heartbeat. The third, lying in her arms, wearing plaid in the eighties, in grey on grey Toronto, being drunk on her words.
MOTHER	If this were my story, it would begin far from here. It would begin at the beginning when I wasn't sure how things would end.
ANNA	This is my story and this is the part where I couldn't get rid of lice
MADELYN	The way you can tell a lice itch from a normal itch is that a lice itch itches a second longer.
ANNA	I found out I had lice in grade six.
MADELYN	Um Anna…
ANNA	Yes, Madelyn
MADELYN	Anna, can I talk to you for a moment?
ANNA	We are talking, Madelyn
MADELYN	Right… I think…
ANNA	Yes Madelyn
MADELYN	I'm…. It's just… I just… I just, I think… I think I just…
ANNA	What is it Madelyn?

MADELYN	I'd feel better about hanging around you…. If you could…
ANNA	Could what?
MADELYN	If maybe…
ANNA	Yes?
MADELYN	If you could check—
ANNA	If I could check what?
MADELYN	If I…
ANNA	If you—
MADELYN	If I could…
ANNA	If you could—
MADELYN	If I could check your head
ANNA	If you could check my head for what?
MADELYN	I've just seen. I might have seen. I have seen—
ANNA	Madelyn please—
MADELYN	You have lice!
ANNA	What?
MADELYN	Lice
ANNA	Lice?
MADELYN	Parasites that live on your head…. Lice. They live in your hair and feed on the blood of your scalp.

ANNA	That's disgusting. That is truly disgusting. They live off your blood?
MADELYN	It just needs attention
ANNA	Are you sure? I mean, are you sure I have them?
MADELYN	Kind of. I mean, I've seen them
ANNA	Really?
MADELYN	Yeah, and I know lice. I had it in grade two. My mother cut off all my hair, it was curly then and it grew back straight. Completely straight.
ANNA	Are you serious? Oh my God I'm never cutting my hair!
MADELYN	That was her first mistake. Can I check you?
ANNA	Okay.

MADELYN starts separating ANNA's hair into sections. Very systematic and very organized.

	I met Madelyn in grade three. She invited me to her Japanese tea party
MADELYN	My mother made me
ANNA	She said I had to bring a Japanese doll
MADELYN	I had read that it was custom for Japanese girls to drink the tea with their dolls
ANNA	My doll was fat
MADELYN	No, just not customary. Hers was—
ANNA	Fat

MADELYN   No, it was this toddler, this plump, plastic toddler doll that only came in a sitting position. It wasn't—

ANNA   Slim

MADELYN   Standing in proper fashion and tiny

MADELYN & ANNA
We didn't like each other

MADELYN   Then Anna had me over

ANNA   My mother made me

MADELYN   We played amusement park

ANNA   I liked more physical games

MADELYN   She locked me in their buffet

ANNA   It was a haunted house

MADELYN   And pounded on it

ANNA   It was supposed to be scary.

MADELYN   I found one!

ANNA   Oh my gosh! Let me see, let me see it. Ew, ew, ew

MADELYN   I—oh shit! *(She drops it.)* I dropped—

ANNA   Ahhhh! *(screaming)* Oh God. Where did it go? Oh God. Oh God. Oh God. Madelyn, where did it go?

MADELYN   There. There it is, no, no that's just another one—

ANNA screams in the "girl sees mouse" fashion.

They are both freaking out, trying to find the missing louse.

ANNA	Where did it go! No, for real Maddy, where did it go!
MADELYN	It's okay, it can only live twenty-four hours outside of the head without dying, don't worry.
ANNA	Oh. *(Her tone changes completely.)* Oh that is so sad. I wonder what it will do. Poor little guy all on its own
MADELYN	I wouldn't worry too much, there's a lot more where that one came from. Yeah Anna, you're pretty loaded. You're like growing a lice farm.
ANNA	Oh God. Get them off. Get them off me. Get them off! Ohhh!
MADELYN	They'll have to be picked out, one by one. And you need the lice shampoo, this special shampoo that's just for lice. Until then…
ANNA	For the next two years Madelyn wore protective gear.

> *MADELYN puts her hair into a tight bun. She puts on a shower cap, a handkerchief, and applies Vaseline to her hairline and sprays her head with an aerosol can.*

MADELYN	They can't attach themselves if it's slippery.

> *She begins picking ANNA's hair. She picks each hair separately, pulling from the root of the hair to the end.*

ANNA	I told my parents
MADELYN	You should know…
ANNA	Well. They're artists. So…
MADELYN	Thorough they are not.

> *MOTHER and FATHER come out and loosely grab two sections of ANNA's hair. MADELYN is still picking in the middle, the parents on either side of her.*

ANNA There are wonderful things about having artists as parents. They are very open.

MADELYN They sponge-painted all the rooms in their house instead of using a normal brush. They think like that.

> *Both parents let go of ANNA's hair.*

ANNA My father did mornings.

DAD Morning sunshine!

ANNA My mother did emotions.

MOTHER Punch this pillow like it is your rage unleashing.

> *ANNA walks over to MOTHER.*

ANNA My mother.

> *ANNA touches her MOTHER's shoulder as if she might disappear.*

MADELYN Lice was the witch hunt of grade two. I got it secretly twice and publicly once, and it was horrifying. It is what my hell would be, always having lice and all food being cappuccino flavoured. You had to cut your hair in stages. You couldn't go from long to short or else people would—

> *MADELYN and ANNA pointing.*

MADELYN & ANNA Lice!

MADELYN   Lice has existed as long as humankind has. Like, in
            the fifteenth century, the Incas, they lived in a soci-
            ety where everyone paid taxes; even the poor who had
            nothing had to pay something. So they would collect all
            the lice off their heads and offer them up as payment.

            *MADELYN places the MOTHER and FATHER's hands
            on ANNA's hair. Her MOTHER and FATHER sit half-
            heartedly picking ANNA's hair.*

ANNA   The shampoo smells like—

MOTHER   Chemicals. *(MOTHER reading bottle)* There are so
            many chemicals. Read this, honey. Oh come here *(to
            FATHER)*, look at this, I've never heard of Nixoci— I
            am not putting chemicals on my daughter's head that I
            can't pronounce. I don't know if we should let her use
            this. I don't believe in these chemicals. And so close
            to the head… you know: the mind. I don't know.
            Honey, read this with me. Look. I've never seen so
            many toxins. The head is a sensitive place, right? We
            can't use this, right? Tell me we can't use this

FATHER   We can't use this? But it is used to kill the lice. People
            use it when they have lice. I think it might be a good
            idea, just because, well—she has lice. I mean it says to
            use the shampoo, right? If you have lice, use the—

MOTHER   I'm not understanding your point.

FATHER   Well, if it says to use the—maybe not. You're right,
            they are harsh chemicals. I just thought it can't be that
            bad if lots of people use it.

MOTHER   I hear what you're saying but I think you're wrong. A
            lot of people use a lot of things that are bad…. I know:
            tea-tree oil. That'll do it, tea-tree oil.

>*MOTHER and FATHER start scratching their own heads. FATHER drops ANNA's hair and whispers to MOTHER. MOTHER walks away, FATHER goes after her.*

ANNA   What's the sound of things going wrong?

>*Everyone whispers like they are conspiring against ANNA.*

I think I still have lice.

>*Everyone whispers like they are conspiring against ANNA.*

My house sometimes gets so quiet.

AUNT   I could tell things weren't— I'm an aunt and a sister; it's my job to waltz in and out and see things. It's my job to say something funny or mean or real. Both my daughters had lice. Both blonds; harder to see the nits on blonds. Melissa—the younger daughter, the happier one, the one who was always hugging people— she got it twice. We'd watch horror films—slasher, bloody, don't-go-up-the-stairs-you-idiot horror flicks. We'd watch them while I nit picked their little blond heads. It made the movies less scary for me and the lice less scary for them. I liked it when they had lice; we'd get to just sort of hang out. My daughters never loved hanging out with me, they were like twins. People would say, "You're so lucky your girls get along so well, do they ever fight?" They fight... with me. My sister and I were close too, but we fought a lot. We fought for our father's attention, our mother's love, the better bed at the cottage. We never felt equal. We liked everything different. Style, movies, books, the taste of dinner. The only thing we did the same and liked the same was getting sick. We would always get sick at the same time. If she sneezed or felt feverish, I'd sneeze and feel feverish. And then we'd both get tucked in and get juice with bendy straws and kisses on our foreheads. We were always equally sick. I'd throw up, she'd throw up. My father would say to my mother, "They get sick together 'cause you always dressed them up in those matching skirts when they were little." Getting sick together was sometimes the only thing we did together.

MADELYN   The suspicion.

ANNA   I got kicked out of school I had lice so bad. Oh yeah, I was hard-core. I was a lice machine. My mother's natural approach didn't work. The principal pulled me aside on my way to gym class. She told me to wait in her room. The only time I was ever sent to the principal's office. I knew something was wrong when I heard—

EVERYONE   Whisper. Whisper.

MADELYN   Whispering never means good things

ANNA   Unless it's a surprise birthday party

MADELYN   But even then it's usually bad. You're not in the mood for a party but you still have to act so grateful

ANNA   Or your hair is flat, and you feel ugly.

Everyone whispers like they are conspiring against ANNA.

I knew I was a good kid. I did extra stuff, like sell hot dogs sometimes, and I shelved books at the library. I had friends; we'd walk around the playground denying crushes.

MADELYN	But like if you had to, if the world was ending and you had to choose a male to procreate with, who would it be in our class?
ANNA	I guess Jamie. If I had to. If the world was ending.
MADELYN	You like Jamie!
ANNA	No. I just think we'd have strong children
MADELYN	I knew it, oh my God!
ANNA	To carry on the human race.... I was athletic, well I long-jumped. I could, I could jump really... long. Unfortunately I was the only girl who didn't shave her legs, so I had to quit due to humiliation but I was a good student, all my projects had a collage element. So when I was asked to wait inside the principal's office.... I thought. (*She sits, looking around nervously.*) Oh my God, my parents are dead. That is the only logical explanation of why *I* would be waiting in the *principal's* office. I'm a good kid. My family has been killed in a car crash, and they don't know how to tell me. So I'm waiting here while they get a professional bad-news teller. Oh God. The house burnt down. My cat! No one saved the cat. Oh God. I'm an orphan and I don't even have a cat! I'll have to be sent away to boarding orphan school and scrub floors, in England scrubbing floors eating only boarding-school mush. (*beat*) I wonder if I'll get to wear a uniform?
PRINCIPAL	Hello Anna
ANNA	Is everything okay? Please tell me someone thought of my cat!

PRINCIPAL	What? Your cat…. We've called your parents to come get you
ANNA	Thank God, what a relief, I was so wor— Am I in trouble?
PRINCIPAL	Oh God, I can see them
ANNA	*(scratching)* See what?
PRINCIPAL	Oh Jesus. Look at them
ANNA	*(scratching)* Look at what?
PRINCIPAL	Lice. You have lice. I mean, it has been reported that you are carrying lice. You're a lice carrier. We are going to ask you to leave the school until you have fully dealt with this situation. You can return to school when the nurse gives you a pass. A no-lice pass. She's checking another school right now.
ANNA	Oh
PRINCIPAL	Cutbacks
ANNA	Oh.
PRINCIPAL	We're sending handouts home with the students so everyone in the school can have a thorough search done at home with their parents
ANNA	Oh God.
PRINCIPAL	Your class is getting checked as we speak. We take the no-lice pass very seriously.
ANNA	I was escorted out.
MADELYN	Oh God, this is terrible

14

BOY	I know. You know, I know the person who outed her
MADELYN	Let's just keep it between us
BOY	Makes sense. I saw her house last year at her birthday party. I saw dirt in the air, like when the sun shines through air, and then there was dust, and stuff, like dust.
ANNA	And I left. No press conference, no editorial, no note to the reader. No nothing to defend myself. Guilty and lousy as charged. I left for three weeks and began an intense nit-picking process at home. I swear I'm not a dirty beast.
MADELYN	It really has nothing to do with dirt. Lice actually prefer clean hair. Better living conditions.

> *MOTHER and FATHER begin nit picking, both pulling at ANNA's hair as they argue.*

MOTHER	She was kicked out of school. I didn't know they could do that. Is that legal, to kick them out of school like that?
FATHER	For how long?
MOTHER	Until she gets rid of the lice, honey. Until they decide she has no lice.
ANNA	They have a nurse
MOTHER	Yeah, they are calling in some so-called nurse. Our daughter has to be, has to be inspected to be let back in to her own school. What year is this? Jesus. I mean, kicked out of public school. She has a right to her education. Every child, lousy or not…

FATHER   We should have used the shampoo

MOTHER   I knew you were going to put this one on me. Who has been the one nit picking her hair for the last seven months?

FATHER   I'm not putting anything on you. I'd be glad to pick nit her—

MOTHER   Nit pick.

FATHER   Yeah.

He takes hold of ANNA's hair. He awkwardly tries.

What am I looking for exactly?

MOTHER   Oh give me that. See, you don't even know how to begin. I told you. Give me that hair

FATHER   It's not my fault she still has lice, I don't know why you are talking to me like this is somehow my big screw-up

ANNA   Well. Mom, what did people do when you were little when someone got lice?

MOTHER   Only poor people got lice then.

Both parents pull back and forth on her head like a tug-of-war.

FATHER   Just show me how to do it, teach me.

MOTHER   You pick from the root of the hair along the hair shaft till the end. You know what the shaft of the hair is right?

FATHER	Yes. Okay. I get it. *(He tries one pick.)* This is easy. *(He does another one.)* And how many hairs do I have to do?
MOTHER	All of them
FATHER	What?
ANNA	Are we poor?
MOTHER	Yes
FATHER	Hey!
MOTHER	We are. What, you don't think we're poor?
FATHER	Is that an attack on me? This is about money now, how I'm in a band and I make so little money
MOTHER	What? No. I find that insulting, it's the twenty-first century. I'm also making us poor. What do you think? You think you're the only one bringing in not enough money?
FATHER	Why are you so angry at me?
ANNA	Why can't rich people get lice?
FATHER	They sure as hell can
MOTHER	I'm not angry at you, I'm just not feeling very— *(She breathes and looks at ANNA.)* Tired. I'm feeling tired. I meant, when I was little we only thought poor people got head lice. It was a classist thing, anyone can get lice
ANNA	A what thing?
FATHER	Honey, are you okay?

MOTHER	A way of people being cruel to each other.
FATHER	Maybe you should lie down. I'll make you some tea, you just relax. I can do this. I can
ANNA	What about you, Dad?
FATHER	We didn't get lice in the prairies. Too cold. *(to the MOTHER)* You want me to do this? I'll try, okay? I think I get it, pull from the hair shaft down, right? You lay down. Sweetie?

They are pulling back and forth on ANNA's hair.

MOTHER	No, I'm fine, you're, you're too sloppy. Those big hands wouldn't be able to. It's a delicate operation.
FATHER	What, this is my hands fault now too? My hands are too big for lice, my eyes are too small, and I make no money.
MOTHER	No... I'm just exhausted. I'm just really, really, really tired of... lice, and I don't think I can do this.
FATHER	It'll be all right.
MOTHER	I'm scared.

FATHER goes to hold MOTHER.

I'm sorry I said all those.... I'm just so—

FATHER	Okay. Oh honey, it's okay. Oh baby. Let's get you into bed. I'll make you some tea.

He lets go of the hair and takes the MOTHER's hand. They walk away.

ANNA is left itching.

MADELYN	The Realization. You still have them
ANNA	Still
MADELYN	You have to go back to school. You're living in exile
ANNA	My parents are trying. They really are. They're trying their best but my mom's really tired and my dad's really busy. He's in a band and he has to play every gig he gets because he's no Mick Jagger. That's what my mom says. My mom paints, and glues things to each other and gets so tired sometimes and then she goes to her bedroom for hours and I don't know what to do. So it's hard. They are trying hard, it's just hard.

Everyone whispers like they are conspiring against ANNA.

And there are secrets and secrets are slippery and it's causing them to fight. And it gets really quiet sometimes in my house, like too quiet. I keep having these dreams about my mom where she is just bleeding and bleeding. Or my dad has been torn apart by wolves. Or my cat has been kidnapped and skinned alive for an art film. I think it's all the blood I'm losing in my head from the lice; it's making me go paranoid.... I don't know why but I just can't get rid of them. I just can't. I can't. I can't. I can't.

She is hitting her head with her hands.

MADELYN	The school advised that she be sent into counselling
ANNA	My parents agreed. They thought therapy never hurt anybody; in fact they were great believers in therapy.
MADELYN	They believed in feeling.

ANNA   As a result, I developed this heightened, very mature, articulate way of speaking.

MADELYN   It was very annoying.

ANNA   Maybe you need to put a boundary around that.

MADELYN   She never felt like I was hearing her.

ANNA   I don't feel like you're hearing me.

MADELYN   I'm not deaf, Anna.

ANNA   I wasn't just in therapy because I had lice. I also had anxiety attacks when my mother left the house. I slept with my legs crossed every night because I was scared of the AIDS monster coming. I prayed. I swallowed my toothpaste because I thought spitting was bad luck. I decided my cat was an indoor cat. You can't go out, Mom, I know you are going to get hit by a car. I can sense it. You can't leave the house, seriously. I can feel it. I had a vision, there was light and then there was darkness and please don't leave

MOTHER   Sweet pea. I'm going to be fine. Please let go of my shirt.

ANNA is dragged across the floor holding onto MOTHER's shirt.

FATHER   Anna, this is ridiculous. Let your mother go

ANNA   No I will not. No, no, no, no.

ANNA itches madly.

MOTHER   Jesus Anna—please tell me you don't still have—

ANNA   I'm sorry

MOTHER	I can't do this anymore— You have to start dealing with this on your own. Really honey, you have to take responsibility, it's too much you know, you need to grow up and—
ANNA	I am grown up, it's just you can't leave 'cause I have this feeling and I forgot to swallow my toothpaste today and I just have this sense, I see colours and, and—
MOTHER	You're talking crazy, Anna. I understand you're scared, but at a certain point you have to start dealing with these feelings on your own. It is not my responsibility to keep getting rid of the lice either, I'm sick of it
ANNA	No of course not, you're way too tired to
FATHER	Anna
ANNA	You know other mothers aren't like you! Madelyn's mother always has energy. She's always doing something, cleaning, and like rearranging the furniture and when Madelyn comes home from school, she makes these little cucumber sandwiches that are really, really good. What do you do all day?
FATHER	Don't talk to your mother like that!
ANNA	What? It's true, Madelyn's mother makes like cookies and stuff and is always the first to volunteer for like, I don't know, everything.
MOTHER	I can't handle this! I will not be guilted. I will not—
ANNA	You're always in bed!
FATHER	That's enough

ANNA
Fine, go, I don't care, leave! I have powers, I see things—but yeah, don't listen to me, just go out and get hit by a car and bleed.

The MOTHER turns away, the FATHER comforts her. ANNA stands alone.

Because of my anxiety attacks my therapist made me close my eyes and recite. "Everything is okay today." *(as therapist)* "Everything is okay today." She was weird. "Just breathe," she'd say. "Anna, breathe." I was like, goddammit I am breathing, if I wasn't breathing I would be dead. "And on the inhale," everything is okay today. She had lipstick a shade darker than it should have been. "Breathe, Anna." It was like her whole face was coloured-in badly. "And on the exhale," everything is okay today. "And close your eyes, travel to your happy place. Anna, are you breathing? Anna, are you in your happy place?" And the room had too much turquoise, you know like someone who has gone to Mexico and they really want you to know... they've gone to Mexico. "And one last time." Actually the whole affair was pretty tacky. "Say it with me." Everything is going to be okay today.

ANNA looks around suddenly to see everyone behind her, alone centre stage.

I had to miss the next appointment because—

MADELYN
Her mother was rushed to the hospital.

ANNA
People think you can hide pain from children. Children just absorb it.

MADELYN
They know when things aren't right. Even if they don't know they know.

ANNA	I never went back to that therapist. She sent me a card once, it stank of sorry. For weeks that's all I could smell, sorry. Everyone reeking sorry. Sorry rooms, full of sorry food, full of people speaking sorry. Cards saying sorry and hands sweating sorry and flowers stinking sorry…
MADELYN	Lice can't drown. When I had lice I would dunk my head in the bath, I thought they couldn't possibly breathe underwater, right? I'd lay for hours in the bath willing the lice away. My brothers would scream, "Maddy's having another bath marathon!"
ANNA	This is my story
MADELYN	So tell it
ANNA	I'm feeling…. I remember I was watching *The Godfather*, part one. I was watching Marlon Brando's mouth full of cotton balls when—

FATHER walks in.

What did the doctors say?

FATHER	What do you mean?
ANNA	I mean at the hospital, what did they say? Is everything okay?
FATHER	We don't… there are tests Anna. We don't know until…. We don't know.
ANNA	Okay, but does everything seem—
FATHER	We just have to wait. I don't— What are you asking me?
ANNA	Dad I… I just want to know—

FATHER   I don't understand what you are asking me!

ANNA   Dad

FATHER   Just don't get all big and upset and…. Anna, please
                don't get all…

ANNA   Yeah.

                Her MOTHER steps forward.

                Both FATHER and ANNA run to her expectantly.

MOTHER   It's going to be okay

FATHER   It's going to be okay.

                MOTHER and FATHER look at each other.

MOTHER   It's going to be okay.

                They all nod together.

ANNA   I never saw *Godfather* part two or three. Okay can
                mean a lot of things, you know.

                They all hold each other.

MADELYN   The Diagnosis.

                FATHER and ANNA in a car.

FATHER   How are you?

ANNA   Fine.

FATHER   And school's going—

ANNA   Fine.

FATHER   You feeling okay?

ANNA	Fine Dad. Okay. I mean I'm feeling okay…. Okay?
	Pause.
FATHER	Do you think Britney had her breasts done?
ANNA	What? Dad, gross! Who cares? …No, she's a teen-ager, they grow. She was fifteen in the "Hit Me Baby One More Time" video.
FATHER	You're right. Poor girl, how horrible to have the world debate your breast size.
ANNA	Dad, she's famous.
FATHER	You mean I don't need to feel bad for her?
ANNA	Dad!
FATHER	Well that's a relief, that's a huge burden off my chest.
ANNA	Dad, I really wouldn't waste my time. There are more important things happening
FATHER	Really?
ANNA	Like in the world
FATHER	Not according to the *Sun*
ANNA	Dad! *(beat)* You read the *Sun*?
FATHER	No! I just saw the front page… and the sports section
ANNA	Dad!
FATHER	I know, it's a guilty pleasure. Anna please, forgive me
ANNA	Like some children have no food, like who the hell cares if Britney Spears had her breasts done or not.

Gosh, you can be so shallow. *(pause)* ...They've had doctors do tests. Plastic surgeons, based on the pictures of her breasts, and they say her breasts, like, hang naturally. So, no I don't think she had them done.

FATHER   Wow. *(silence)* Anna?

ANNA   What?

FATHER   I ah... I wanted to talk to you about.... Tell you...

ANNA   Yes Dad...

FATHER   Ah... I wanted to say—

ANNA   Yes?

FATHER   Don't ever get a breast job

ANNA   Dad!

FATHER   It's not worth it

ANNA   Dad.

FATHER   I'm serious. No breast jobs, and don't dye your hair or get a tattoo.

ANNA   Oh my God

FATHER   Or ride on the back of a boy's motorcycle

ANNA   That's what you want to talk to me about?

FATHER   I'm your father. I care about you

ANNA   And my breasts apparently... Dad

FATHER   Yeah.... Ah.... Well the thing is—

ANNA	What thing?
FATHER	Well, it's nothing to be alarmed about.... It's just... there are probably going to be some people at home when we get there.
ANNA	Okay.
FATHER	Your mother has cancer.
ANNA	Okay.
FATHER	Anna?
ANNA	I know, sort of. I figured. I know, figured, you know?
	Massive pause.
FATHER	...Yeah so this is going to be a bit of a hard time. An okay hard time, but a hard time. We have people to help and support us. We have options. Chemotherapy and.... We have help. Everything's just fine, it's just I wanted you to know
ANNA	Yeah. *(pause)* But I can't make that promise
FATHER	What?
ANNA	That I won't ride on the back of a boy's motorcycle
FATHER	Anna...
ANNA	What? I can't. If he's really hot, I will ride. I will.
	Pause.
FATHER	Everything's just fine, we have options. *(He smiles.)* Okay?
ANNA	Yeah. That's when everyone started borrowing smiles. Borrowed smiles, and furrowed foreheads. Foreheads

are maps to ones emotions because no one thinks of lying in their forehead; no one thinks of covering up those frowns. I thought I could read a forehead better than a mouth. So I watched the foreheads of everybody as they smiled their smiles and all told me:

FATHER   It's going to be okay

ANNA   Yeah, totally. The thing about lice is, if you miss just one louse they escalate, you can do as many treatments as you want. You miss one nit and it just hatches and multiplies. It went so quickly from bad to worse. I could shake my hair, you know, like Ally Sheedy in the *Breakfast Club*, but instead of snow—

MADELYN   Dandruff

ANNA   Instead of dandruff, lice would fall out.

I lived in fear people would find out I had lice again.

AUNT & MADELYN
How's the lice situation?

ANNA   Totally fine, it's fine. Why? What? It's gone. It's just a dry season, my scalp is itchy.

AUNT and MADELYN look at her suspiciously.

My dad never got lice though.

FATHER   It's true.

MADELYN   They don't like men's hair as much, it's a girl thing. Another reason why being a girl is a blast.

FATHER   I never saw the lice. I thought they were invisible. It seemed medieval or something. It seemed... I don't know

ANNA	My father got frustrated.
FATHER	Why don't you just shave your head!
ANNA	I am not going to shave my head, gosh, Dad, you really don't get it do you?
FATHER	Get what?
ANNA	Exactly. Being a girl, Dad. Gosh.
MADELYN	The problem is Anna can't just deal with things. She needs to just pick her hair every day. It's the only way to get rid of it. *(putting on more gear)* I cannot keep getting lice, Anna
ANNA	I know *(itching ferociously)*
MADELYN	I have stuff to do. You know my mom has to keep nit picking my hair too. It's not fair
ANNA	I'm sorry. I'm trying
MADELYN	I know but it's been like—
ANNA	I know but things have been… I'm sorry, I think I might have super lice, like they're undefeatable, like I can't win…. My aunt tried a couple times too
AUNT	I'll get you little bastards. Do you want to rent *Halloween II*?
ANNA	My aunt has a clean house
MADELYN	With fresh Kleenex, always
AUNT	I believe in vacuum cleaners. I believe in dirt being sucked up. Quickly. I believe in Kleenex. I believe in being good to your nose. I believe in things going

away, I believe you can make things go away. Anna is not my daughter but I will get rid of her lice. I will.

AUNT starts nit picking ANNA's hair.

ANNA   I had to stay at my aunt's house because—

FATHER   It's not that chemo didn't work

ANNA   Uh-huh.

FATHER   This is just a natural method

ANNA   Like tea-tree oil.

FATHER   It's this treatment in Mexico for cancer.

ANNA   Mexico?

FATHER   It's called the Grierson diet. It involves a lot of juicing

ANNA   Juicing?

FATHER   We're just going for two weeks. And then we'll do it here, the juicing

ANNA   Juicing?

FATHER   They put you, her, on juice every half-hour from eight in the morning till eight at night.

ANNA   Oh

FATHER   Obviously we'll have to get help, with the juicing. I was thinking of that young poet guy who fixed our fridge. He probably needs the cash, he could probably juice.

ANNA   Juicing is pretty poetic. So they just teach you how to make juice to cure cancer. Cancer-curing juice

FATHER   No there's other stuff too like…. Ah… other stuff

ANNA   Yeah.

FATHER   It's going to be okay. You'll stay with your aunt

ANNA   Yeah

AUNT   We'll go shopping. We'll buy jeans. We'll buy the perfect jeans. She's going to die. She's dying. Don't say it. If this were my story, I'd tell her she's dying. She is. My sister is. I'd scream *my sister is dying, help!* We'll go to the Gap. I know it's bad, but we'll find jeans that fit right there. I'm going to buy you the perfect jeans. The perfect size, the perfect cut, okay?

ANNA   Yeah.

AUNT   My sister's dying of cancer and no one is—

SALESWOMAN
May I help you?

AUNT   We're looking for jeans

ANNA   No we're fine, thanks

SALESWOMAN
Boot cut, flared, slim fit, long and lean, relaxed, or stretched, either black, faded black, denim, dark denim, light denim, faded denim, fresh, or worked in, what size are you looking for today miss?

ANNA   I don't know, I… I don't know…

AUNT   We'll try a couple different types

ANNA   Not tapered and not with those white patches, like you sat in flour or something. And I don't want denim stretch pants. Jeans should be stiff.

AUNT   How about flared? We thought flared was cool when I was young. I can't tell you what it is like to watch what you wore come and go and then come back again. It comes back a little less thrown together though. The hippies aren't as dirty as they were. The shirts aren't as baggy.

ANNA   It must be nice to never worry; you were definitely the most creative generation.

AUNT   No— I wasn't saying— It just makes me feel old

ANNA   I hate salespeople

AUNT   Anna

ANNA   They're horrible.

SALESWOMAN
            I got your daughter some—

AUNT   She's not my daughter, she's my niece. I'm just taking her shopping for jeans. She's my very special niece. She needs very special jeans. She's not my daughter, she has a mother, her own mother, I'm just her aunt. Her special aunt.

SALESWOMAN
            That's nice.

AUNT   My sister is going to die. Try these Anna.

            ANNA is in the dressing room, she is so tired she can barely put one leg in her jeans.

ANNA   They don't fit

AUNT	That's okay. No problem. That's why we came to the Gap. Do you want a different cut or just a different size? How about the colour, too dark, too light, too denim?
ANNA	No, just a different size.

Her AUNT goes to get a new pair. ANNA starts scratching until she is scratching her entire body.

I am so itchy. Everyone is smiling around me, but they should be frowning. I don't understand. They're everywhere. All over. Get off me, get off me. I am so— I just need a moment to catch up. Okay? Just a moment, you know? Figure out what's going on, so I can just understand, realize, assess how upset I am. I just need a moment to get rid of my lice. This itch. I just need—

Pushing the lice off of her.

SALESWOMAN

Do you need any help?

ANNA No!

SALESWOMAN

Another size perhaps?

ANNA Everywhere I go there are words and smiles and kisses and okays. But what I need is a moment, just to catch up, to get rid of these. *(She is scratching herself crazy.)* I feel so... so itchy. Get off. Get off, you assholes, you freaky bugs, you stupid lice. Just go away. Go way, go away, go away

AUNT I have the other—

ANNA	*Go away!*
AUNT	It's me.
ANNA	Oh sorry. I thought it was that twit of a saleswoman.
SALESWOMAN	
	I'm here too.
AUNT	Can I come in, Anna?
ANNA	Yes.
AUNT	Are you on drugs?
ANNA	What?
AUNT	I heard it's a way of escaping.
ANNA	No.

Pause.

AUNT	…Are you bulimic?
ANNA	What?
AUNT	I read it's a way of controlling things.
ANNA	No. I am not bulimic.
AUNT	Oh. That's good. That's very good. Oh dear, I love you so much, Anna. I wish—I just wish I could…. How are you doing? Feeling? *(weeping)* How are you really? How do you really feel?
ANNA	Fine, how do you really feel?
AUNT	I'm…. Well…. Me? I feel, I feel very, I feel…

ANNA	Overwhelmed
AUNT	No… I feel…
ANNA	Scared?
AUNT	No…. Should I be scared?
ANNA	There are no shoulds; you are whatever you are feeling
AUNT	You're right. It's just been hard. It's been hard not… I haven't seen her; I'd like to see her… I just feel really…
ANNA	Confused
AUNT	No… well yes… well maybe. I just—
ANNA	Do you want to punch a pillow?
AUNT	No, well…. No, I just feel… I feel…
ANNA	Come on, let it out
AUNT	I want to buy you jeans!
ANNA	I see. Well it's quite possible that you are having a nervous breakdown. You should just breathe *(ANNA starts scratching.)*
AUNT	No. I'm, I… it's you. *(weeping)* I want you to—you need jeans, I want to buy you the perfect jeans. I'm scared—I'm worried about…. Jeans
ANNA	Just say, "Everything is okay today."
AUNT	I want to—
ANNA	Say it with me

AUNT	I need to see—
ANNA	Shhh, just close your eyes and think of your happy place.
AUNT	My— Oh yes. Okay. Here I go. Yes.

AUNT closes her eyes.

ANNA	Are you in your happy place?
AUNT	Yes. Yes, there is Kleenex everywhere. Yes…

ANNA holds her AUNT's hand. A pause.

Now what?

ANNA	Now we leave the Gap. Everything is going to be okay today.

They walk out. ANNA is still in her underwear.

AUNT	Everything is going to be okay.
SALESWOMAN	
	Excuse me? Miss—
ANNA	No! We're fine! Can't you see we're fine?
SALESWOMAN	
	But your—
ANNA	We don't want to buy jeans!
SALESWOMAN	
	It's just you're forgetting your pants. Miss? You're not wearing any pants.
AUNT	Oh my God. Anna?

ANNA just stands scratching her head in her underwear. A moment.

Anna?

ANNA gets dizzy.

ANNA   Juicing.

She collapses to the ground.

SALESWOMAN
Shit.

AUNT holds ANNA's head in her lap, she caresses it and sees something, she moves in closer.

AUNT   Oh Anna.

ANNA   Yes? *(groggy)*

AUNT   You have lice again.

Her AUNT starts delousing her hair.

Her FATHER comes carrying in her MOTHER.

Everyone whispers like they are conspiring against ANNA.

ANNA   How's she doing?

FATHER   Really well.

He lays her down, she is barely moving. ANNA stares at her.

MADELYN   The Relapse.

ANNA   I was so close to getting rid of the lice while my parents were in Mexico. *(to MADELYN)*

They're gone, I swear

MADELYN   Okay. *(MADELYN puts on a bandana and hugs ANNA, pulling her head away from her.)*

ANNA   And I finally told my friends at school about my mother

FRIEND   Oh my God. You are so brave. You are like... I can't believe it. *(starts crying)* It's just so... oh gosh, I can't, should we go to the girls' washroom?

ANNA   No I don't really want to go cry there. I mean, I think it's going to be okay. I mean, thank you, but please don't cry

FRIEND   Your right. Oh sweetie, it's totally okay, see my cousin's boyfriend's aunt had cancer of the—what kind of cancer is it? Your mom's, what's her cancer?

ANNA   Um, well—

FRIEND   My cousin's boyfriend's aunt had toe cancer and we were all like freaked, of course, but then it was so totally fine... so... it's, what I'm saying is, it's going to be so totally fine, okay?

ANNA   Okay. It's just sometimes hard, you know?

FRIEND   Yeah, but like no one said cancer was easy. No one goes like, "Gee, I really want cancer"

ANNA   I wasn't saying—

FRIEND   It's going to be fine, I just know it. Like yesterday I was thinking, *Whatever happened to Ricky Martin?* And then I turn on MuchMusic and there is like this special called *Where Did Ricky Martin's Bon Bon Shake To?* I

	was like, oh my God, I'm psychic. Ooooh you are so brave! If you need to talk to anybody I'm really here, I'm totally here, for you, I'm here for you, okay?
ANNA	What I really needed was some tongue. See all my fear went one place when my mother was sick. My crotch was in a state of swollen anticipation.
FATHER	So. We've kinda hired this poet guy to help with the juicing for the summer
ANNA	Kinda? Right. *(to MADELYN)* I hope he's cute
MADELYN	I hope he can play cards.
FATHER	I'm here. I'm here for her. This is what I can do, be here. And prop pillows. *(He goes propping pillows around the MOTHER.)* She asked me—
MOTHER	I just don't want them to see me like this
FATHER	They love you, they just want—
MOTHER	I can't—
FATHER	I understand completely
MOTHER	I just want to concentrate on getting better. Drinking juice and being healed. I can't stand the idea of their thoughts when they leave me. What they'll say to each other. I can't
FATHER	What about your sister?
MOTHER	Oh… I just need some space from that concern, I don't want her to… it's just for a little while…. While I concentrate on the juicing and healing, just tell her I'm tired and doing fine, I'm doing fine

FATHER   You are

MOTHER   I am. Just immediate family right now and— Madelyn?

MADELYN   I was—sorry. I was looking for Anna

MOTHER   Oh she's trying on clothes for the poet's arrival

MADELYN   Sorry

MOTHER   Don't be. I haven't seen you in a while

MADELYN   Four months

MOTHER   You've grown so much. You are so beautiful, Madelyn, you have grown into such a beautiful young woman

MADELYN   No

MOTHER   Yes. I'm sorry we haven't seen more of each other this year. Are you still painting? You used to paint all the time. It's so good for Anna to have you; a friend that finally got her hands dirty, and colourful. You still paint? High school hasn't crushed that out of you? You haven't changed your focus to the colours of lip gloss I hope

MADELYN   No, not yet.... Do you want to see some? I have a couple of paintings here, but—

MOTHER   Oh yes. Yes I do.

MADELYN shows her a book of her drawings.

Oh Madelyn. These are beautiful. Beautiful. Beautiful. You are really good. You are. Wow. I love this one with all the hair... turning into... the sea

MADELYN   Thanks.

MOTHER	And this one here, of the pregnant woman. So golden and full. You have gotten so good; you have such an imaginative sense of colour.
MADELYN	Well, I learnt it from you, you told me last summer to try playing more with colours
MOTHER	Yes, last summer.
MADELYN	Yeah, I should go. You're probably really tired
MOTHER	Can I have this painting of the pregnant woman? This one in yellow
MADELYN	Yes. Of course.
MOTHER	You should take my watercolours. Over there, and my easel too for a while.
MADELYN	No. I couldn't, you need them
MOTHER	And my brushes. Just for the summer, it's okay. I want you to have them.
MADELYN	Okay. Thanks
MOTHER	You do look very beautiful, Madelyn. Very grown-up. You are your own little woman.
MADELYN	Sh-sh-hh-sh... I started working on her face. Shhhh, a painting of her face just for myself. Sh-sh-hh.... Just for myself. Just in yellow.... My mother doesn't like colour, we have a very white house, my mother gets overwhelmed easily. She likes there to be room to breathe. Space. She'll often say, "I want more space. Let's make this more spacious. I need space." I love clutter, I love filling my room with memories and wrappers, tissues and bus tickets.... When I told my

mom I first got my period, she said, "And so it begins." Anna's mom took Anna and I out for dinner to celebrate our womanhood, she gave us purses and diaries. She said that our power was in how we think, and how we carry our power is our sexuality. I think my mother finds being a woman messy, which I don't get because I have three brothers, talk about messy. I have three brothers and when I try to describe them I feel stuffy and overheated. My mom would de-lice my hair every time I got lice. None of my brothers ever got lice, just me. I am the girl. I get lice. Again and again. So I developed this system. It's important to have systems in place to deal with things; my mother and father are good at systems. You can't raise four kids without systems. You need a plan, like painting, there are steps, sections, you do things.... I will finish this painting, part by part, piece by piece. You have to have a plan. The treatment—

POET   Hey

ANNA   Hey

MADELYN   Hey

ANNA   You're the poet.

POET   I guess, I'm here to help with the cooking and, uh... juicing

ANNA   Do you want to play cards?

POET   Sure. Why not?

MADELYN   Kings in the Corner

ANNA   Yeah

POET	I don't know—
MADELYN	We'll teach you
ANNA	We're good at that.
MADELYN	So.
ANNA	You have a girlfriend?
POET	Yeah
ANNA	Is she…
MADELYN	Nice?
POET	I guess
ANNA	Nice-nice?
POET	I don't know—
MADELYN	You don't know if she's nice—
ANNA	Nice.
POET	Well I think she's nice
ANNA	Would you say she's cute, hot, pretty, beautiful, or sexy?
POET	Well she's all these things at different times to me
ANNA	Please
MADELYN	Well aren't you a lucky man

MADELYN & ANNA
Come on

ANNA	If you had to

MADELYN	Had to-had to
ANNA	At gunpoint
POET	*(coughing)* Man. Okay. I'd say she's… sexy?
ANNA	Sexy cute?
MADELYN	Does she pout? Mmm-mmm. *(MADELYN does exaggerated pouting with her lips.)*
POET	Well…
ANNA	Is she sexy hot?
MADELYN	Does she let it all hang out?
ANNA	Oh, oh sorry, did you just see my nipple? Sorry, wardrobe malfunction *(imitating someone large breasted falling out)*
POET	No, she's not—
MADELYN	Is she pretty sexy?
ANNA	Oops I did it again… I'm sexy? What, this is my school uniform?
POET	Maybe…
ANNA	Or organic sexy?
MADELYN	I let my armpit hair grow out, I'm sexy with the confidence I have in not trying to be sexy.
POET	Yes that's it!
ANNA	Oh
MADELYN	Oh

ANNA	Let's play cards
MOTHER	Anna, come in here. Anna
ANNA	What?
MOTHER	I can see your children.
ANNA	Ah, okay
MOTHER	I can see what they look like, my grandchildren. Little, round, soft faces
ANNA	Mom you're—why are you holding Madelyn's picture?
MOTHER	Beautiful babies, I'll see them. I'm not worried about that…

ANNA scratches ferociously.

ANNA	You know a lot of the time Madelyn traces stuff
MOTHER	Little, round, soft faces.
ANNA	Do you like my pants? I got them yesterday
MOTHER	I will hold my grandchildren. I know I will
ANNA	Mom, I want your honest opinion on them, I'm going to walk for you and I want you to pay extra attention to the bum, this is important, watch
MOTHER	Anna
ANNA	Do you like them, Mom?
MOTHER	Yes. Very cute
ANNA	I'm so not going for cute.

FATHER   I'm…. It wasn't like when I first saw her everything stopped and there were fireworks. It wasn't like when I first looked at her the world stopped moving. No, it was the opposite of that actually. When I first met her my life began moving. I was no longer trying to catch up, suddenly I was a part of something much greater than me… I'm… I'm…. Sometimes she catches me staring at her, she squints her eyes and says, "What? What is it?" And I say what I'm supposed to say, "You're so beautiful." See how well-trained I am…? But really what I'm thinking when I look at her is… we are just waiting till our vanity runs out… we are just buying time till we get old…. I'm… I'm scared. Not that my life will stop after she… no… I'm scared that it will keep going, going until suddenly…. I'm scared of getting old. I'm so scared of being old without her…. I called everyone. What about your sister? Are you still up for seeing your sister?

MOTHER   No… I can't right now

FATHER   She's left five messages

MOTHER   I said I can't.

FATHER   She said she's coming

MOTHER   Honey I don't feel like you are hearing me, I can't see her right now

FATHER   She just wants to, people just want to—

MOTHER   Say goodbye

FATHER   That's not what I was going to say

MOTHER   I will not spend my energy making them feel better about me being sick

Scratch

FATHER	Of course, I'll call your sister again. I wasn't saying that, I wasn't going to say that. I have to go to work. I love you. I love you, my beautiful wife. *(kisses her)*
AUNT	I have bendy straws and Kleenex, where is she?
FATHER	You didn't get my message
AUNT	It's nice to see you too, you look good, well you look… I'm here
FATHER	Oh…. Well the thing is, she's, I left you a message. I didn't… she's… she's not seeing people right now.
AUNT	I'm her sister
FATHER	Yes
AUNT	I don't understand
FATHER	Well, the thing is… she's… it's just, she's a little on the tired side of things, you know
AUNT	I have bendy straws
FATHER	Yes
AUNT	I'm going to see her
FATHER	She's tired— She wants to be alone, soon she'll see you soon. She wants to see you when she's better
AUNT	Better?
FATHER	…Yes… better…
AUNT	Tell her I'm here, I'm her sister and I'm here to be with her
FATHER	I ah… I don't think—

47

AUNT	Just tell her
FATHER	It's not that, well it's just not a good time
AUNT	This is ridiculous; I'm going in there
FATHER	No. The thing is… you see, it's hard but she, well, she isn't—
AUNT	Just speak goddammit.
FATHER	She doesn't want to see you!
AUNT	Oh…
FATHER	I'm sorry… I'll get her to call you when she's…
AUNT	Better…. Well I guess I'll just leave these things here, yes, I got her this Kleenex box with roses on it—it's kitsch, I know—but she loves roses and I wanted, it's good quality—the Kleenex, with lotion in it—I don't know how they do it, I'm just glad there are people who care enough to—take the time to—I'll just. I'll leave this
FATHER	I'm sorry
POET	Your juice and breakfast
MOTHER	Oh. Thank you. Oh this, this is heavenly. Mmmm. This is like snowflakes on the tongue, but with taste. Thank you. Thank you.

POET smiles.

POET	The sickness seems to heighten the life. It's like being on the edge of something and it's dangerous. Being so close to something…

MADELYN	But so removed.
POET	I wrote poems
MADELYN	You are a poet.
POET	I wrote poems about anticipation. The taste of living, the smell of dying... and girls giggling. I wrote poems about juice, peeling the skins off of apples, smelling orange peel on my palms. The sound of her chewing. An entire poem on the sound of her chewing.
MADELYN	Sounds great
POET	It is going to be... it's going to be beautiful. Feeding someone is so intimate
MOTHER	Mmmm. Oh this is divine. This potato is perfect. A perfect potato, bravo. Bravo!

The POET hands her another plate.

Steamed kale. Oh yes.

He hands her another plate.

Squash. Oh God. Cinnamon squash.

POET	Feeding someone is like making love to someone slowly.
MOTHER	This feels.... This tastes so good
POET	But better. Because it nourishes them. If this was my story, it would be... an epic poem
MADELYN	It would be boring.
POET	My girlfriend has bad circulation. Her hands and toes are always cold, as if half of her is grabbing, reaching,

stuck in another time. I have always attracted bird-like women who flutter and coo, and when angered squawk and fly away. The only thing gentle about my girlfriend is her orgasms. She was starved when I met her, starved for love and protein and I fed her and I loved her and she hates me for it. She hates me for filling her. My girlfriend is hard while everyone here is just so...

MADELYN   Exposed.

POET   I'm feeling so much. It's hard to keep track...

MADELYN   Of what belongs to you. *(POET itches his head.)*

POET   She is just so beautiful, sometimes I just watch her lips. "Her lips are her life...." "Life/lips...." There's something there.

MADELYN   *(sarcastically)* Yeah, definitely.

ANNA   Want to play cards?

POET   I have to make her lunch. I'm sautéing the kale in carrot juice; I'm going to make a feast out of so little. I've seasoned the potatoes just right. I want to watch her lips... I want to make her...

ANNA   What?

POET   Mouth water

ANNA   Well I want to play cards

POET   Does she like Newfoundland salmon?

ANNA   I don't know if she can eat that

POET   Oh

ANNA	There are like these… she's on a very strict diet. You should really check if she can eat salmon before you go through all that trouble
POET	I know, I just… I want to…
ANNA	Go see your girlfriend. *(ANNA leaves.)*
POET	Yeah. But she is so—
GIRLFRIEND	What's it like?
POET	Full, very full, there are so many feelings—
GIRLFRIEND	Yeah. What about the girl?
POET	She's nice, dealing well
GIRLFRIEND	Is she ugly?
POET	What?
GIRLFRIEND	Can you see the tumour?
POET	I don't—
GIRLFRIEND	What does it look like?
POET	Like she's pregnant
GIRLFRIEND	Oh God
POET	But tender
GIRLFRIEND	Oh God
POET	Maybe I shouldn't tell you these things—
GIRLFRIEND	Kiss me.

He does.

Is the young girl pretty?

POET I don't know

GIRLFRIEND Well do you find her pretty?

POET Yeah she looks like her mother

GIRLFRIEND So the mother *is* pretty

POET Well she's very sick

GIRLFRIEND That can be hot

POET God

GIRLFRIEND What?

POET You can be so cold and hard, like part of you is frozen, afraid, hardened by time

GIRLFRIEND Wow. You sure have a way with words. So is she dying beautifully, are you overcome by the beauty of it all?

POET …You know I was thinking maybe you could talk to the girl, about what you went through with your dad. I know you don't talk that much about it but it might be good for her and you, you know healing?

> *GIRLFRIEND takes POET's hand and puts it on her breast.*

GIRLFRIEND I wore pink with purple Doc Martens to my father's funeral, hot pink—a big fuck you to black. I remember every party, function, little gathering of friends at the time, I could draw this line connecting every grief in the room to each other and then back to me. Connect the grief

POET   Connect the grief, wow...

GIRLFRIEND   *(She laughs at him.)* Yeah... I remember this one gathering vividly, I wore this fuchsia dress that looked like an upside-down tulip, and literally everyone who had lost someone in their life came up to me and, holding their grief tightly, they'd stare, right at my face, like it was their reflection. "I know it's not the same," they'd say. "I'm not trying to compare." But I knew, even at eleven. *Yes, yes you are.* We are all sizing up each other's grief. There is this elitism to the ones that carry tragedy, and early on we learn how to carry our grief. How to accessorize it.

POET   Oh... wow...

GIRLFRIEND   If I talked to her, it would be about me, my story, I don't know her. Okay? There is nothing I can say, there is nothing to say.

POET   It's so beautiful to watch you open up to me, awaken— I feel like I am seeing you for the first time

GIRLFRIEND   Oh please—these are just words. That's the problem with poetry. What, you think words are honest? You want tragedy? Watch me put on a sweater, or eat my Corn Flakes, true tragedy lives in the ordinary, not in poetry. Enjoy your beautiful tragedy while it lasts.

ANNA   Did you see your girlfriend?

POET   Yeah actually... Anna?

ANNA   Yes?

POET   My girlfriend's father died of prostate cancer

ANNA   Okay

POET	When she was eleven
ANNA	Bummer
POET	Yeah…
ANNA	Okay
POET	I thought maybe you and her could… it doesn't matter—hey you want to play that game later, Kings in the Corner?
ANNA	Me and her could what?
POET	I was going to say get along, hang out or something.
ANNA	If she likes cards like you do, I'm sure we would.
POET	How are you doing?
ANNA	Fine, great, horrible. Why?
POET	I just worry about you
ANNA	Okay
POET	How you're doing and things. I just want you to know I care about you, and you can talk to me. Anna, I know things are… I just wanted you to know I'm a very good listener.
ANNA	That's great for you, but I'm looking for a kiss. See I need to be kissed very, very soon. With tongue.

She stares right at him.

POET	I should bring the salmon to your mother
ANNA	You should cook the salmon first

POET	I should cook the salmon for your mother
ANNA	Yeah you should.
	Pause.
POET	You look so much like her
ANNA	I hope so, she's my mother
POET	You're both very beautiful
ANNA	We're in pain. People have to be beautiful if they are in pain, it's only fair, right?
POET	You'll get your kiss.
ANNA	Yeah, well it better happen soon. Very, very soon.
	She stares right at him, scratching intensely but casually.
	Well, I guess I'll let you go back to your... salmon and... stuff
POET	Yeah
ANNA	See you later. *(beat)* Do you think the poet is cute?
MADELYN	In a needy way
ANNA	I think he was checking me out yesterday
MADELYN	That's disgusting.
ANNA	Why? You think I'm not check-outable?
MADELYN	No. Yes. Of course I do. It's just he's taking care of your mother
ANNA	He's cooking for her. He's hired help

MADELYN	Anna
ANNA	What? He is, we're paying him to cook and look cute
MADELYN	He was hired for his skills.
ANNA	And his cuteness. I think he has a crush on my mom
MADELYN	She's really beautiful
ANNA	And I'm not?
MADELYN	No. I just meant he's taking care of her and she's really beautiful, so it must seem like he has a crush on her, anyways I don't think you should be joking about these things
ANNA	Why?
MADELYN	This is a serious time
ANNA	Oh okay Maddy.
MADELYN	…I mean, yeah he's cute…. Sh-sh-hh-shh. I've been working on painting her face, all in yellows like Picasso's blue period. Madelyn's yellow period. I know she's not my mother, but she is my…. I have a shrine dedicated to her health. It's got a picture of her and some flowers and my favourite paintings in postcard versions and these tiny Japanese parasols that come off fancy drinks. Everything pretty around her picture. I'm going to paint the perfect portrait…. I check my hair every night on my own. I have a system. I comb through it with the nit comb, and I spray it, and put Vaseline all over. I don't care if my hair always looks greasy. It's a system and it works. When I go out, I keep it hidden; I wrap it in coloured scarves, and knitted hats. At night I unwrap and stare at it.

My hair, I am the only one that gets to see it. It's a tiring system, but it's satisfying. If this was my story, it wouldn't be about lice.

ANNA is still scratching her head.

ANNA and MADELYN watch as the FATHER, with the AUNT and the POET, carry the MOTHER to the other side of the room.

Anna

ANNA   I know. I have it again.

MADELYN   It's okay

ANNA   I'm sorry

MADELYN   It's okay, we'll deal with it… later.

They hug, avoiding each other's heads.

She was taken

FATHER   She was brought… uh… we admitted…

ANNA   Her to the hospital. The summer was over. Fall was…

MADELYN   Everything turned colour and smell and taste. Everything turned.

POET   I started working on the poem. I think it might be my best one… I'm calling it "Pain"… I think…. That or "Loss at the End of Summer"

MADELYN   Oh God

ANNA   The hospital was too clean. It is a place for the sick, but it was too clean, too clean for the sick. I want more than anything—

MADELYN	A boyfriend.
ANNA	When my mother was put into—rushed into the hospital. I was very overwhelmed
MADELYN	You were very horny
ANNA	I had a lot of feelings
MADELYN	And most of them went to one place
ANNA	Madelyn!
MADELYN	It's true.
ANNA	I wanted a distraction
MADELYN	A boystraction
FATHER	Anna
ANNA	Yes. *(scratching pretty hard)* Dad, I need to talk to you
FATHER	Yes. *(scratching)* I need to talk to you too
ANNA	I think—
FATHER	We need to—

They scratch furiously together.

ANNA	Sorry. You go
FATHER	No. No, you go. *(scratching building)*

ANNA and FATHER speak at the same time.

ANNA	I have lice again and maybe we should check you too because—

FATHER	Your mother probably is probably not going to… probably make it.
ANNA	Oh…

A voluptuous pause.

FATHER	Anna…
ANNA	Where's my aunt?
FATHER	She's there already
ANNA	She's seeing people now?
FATHER	Some people. Come let's go see her…. Anna—come on, let's go together. I'll drive us
ANNA	No
FATHER	I know, it's going to be hard, but—
ANNA	I'll go later. I'll see you there later
FATHER	Anna
ANNA	I'll see you there… later

ANNA goes to scratch her head and stops.

So my mother is probably going to die.

MADELYN	What?
ANNA	She's probably not going to make it
MADELYN	No.
ANNA	She's very sick

MADELYN	I know that, but I thought she was getting better, I mean she was getting better
ANNA	Yeah, well I just wanted to tell you because you're like my—
MADELYN	Oh my God. No
ANNA	It's okay, Madelyn. It's going to be okay—
MADELYN	No it's not. Oh my God. Are you all right? I mean of course you're not, but are you—
ANNA	I'm fine. I'm doing fine. I've decided to stay at my aunt's. I thinks it's best and all. Are you okay?
MADELYN	No. No I am not okay.
ANNA	Oh.
MADELYN	Can I see her?
ANNA	Right now she's just seeing family.
MADELYN	Oh. Right. Of course…
	Pause.
	How is she?
ANNA	Well she's dying
MADELYN	I mean. Have you seen her?
ANNA	No, not yet.
MADELYN	What?
ANNA	I mean I'm going to, I've been…

MADELYN	You have to go. Anna, you have to—
ANNA	Clearly I am going to go, I'm her daughter, obviously I'm going. She's my mother. I'm going... now actually.
MADELYN	Now
ANNA	Yeah. I'm on my way there actually
MADELYN	Okay. Well.... Tell her I.... Tell her...
ANNA	What?
MADELYN	I dunno, that I.... Tell her I say hi
ANNA	Hi?
MADELYN	No, yes... I don't know. Do you want me to go with you?
ANNA	No. I'll be fine. I'll see you later, Madelyn
MADELYN	Yeah. Later.

ANNA stands alone looking at her reflection, a LITTLE OLD LADY volunteer approaches her.

LITTLE OLD LADY

Excuse me. Miss? Are you lost, miss?

ANNA   Yes. What? No. Who are you?

LITTLE OLD LADY

I work here. Well I volunteer here. I'm a helper

ANNA   Congratulations.

LITTLE OLD LADY

Well... thank you, I mean. I'm—it's a, I get so much out of it myself, it's very—

ANNA   I'm sorry, I didn't mean to make you blush…

LITTLE OLD LADY

I'm not— No… well— Is everything all right? You've been standing outside the elevator for quite some time. Can I help you find anything?

ANNA   I'm trying to find an accurate reflection.

LITTLE OLD LADY

But that's not a mirror, it's a metal elevator door

ANNA   So what do you do exactly? How do you help? You like make sure no one stares too long at an elevator door, you keep an eye out for suspicious things, make sure no one steals a purse, or a baby? *(She laughs.)*

LITTLE OLD LADY

That's not very funny

ANNA   Oh. Sorry.

LITTLE OLD LADY

I do a lot of knitting and—

ANNA   That's cool. I respect that. You help by knitting. The world does need more knit things

LITTLE OLD LADY

Excuse me, I—

ANNA   No I'm serious. I do think a lot of the world's problems could be solved by wool mittens

LITTLE OLD LADY

You're not being very nice

ANNA   I'm sorry. I'm just lost. Is this the maternity ward?

LITTLE OLD LADY
No, this is floor five, the cancer—

ANNA Oh.

LITTLE OLD LADY
Are you not on the right floor miss?

ANNA Yes— No, I am. It's just these blues and pinks: you'd think they'd be colours for babies being born, not for mothers dying, eh? You need a new a decorating scheme. This is where people check in and check out. You want to at least get the colours right.

LITTLE OLD LADY
Oh well, yes, I'll, ah, I'll be sure to let someone know. Can I take you somewhere?

ANNA *(itching her head)* Is there a lice ward?

> POET *enters but, walking and scribbling on a pad of paper, he doesn't see* ANNA.

POET Pain…. Pain pain… it begins and ends in pain. Life/ pain/perfect potatoes…. I'm getting somewhere, definitely, potato slash pain. Potato/pain/pain potato.

(He writes it down.) …Anna

ANNA What are you doing here?

POET Anna? I came… I just wanted to see her

ANNA Why?

POET Well, to say goodbye

ANNA She saw you?

POET	No. She is just seeing—
ANNA	Family.
POET	Yeah. I don't know why I came really, I guess I missed—
ANNA	Making her food. *(nervously)* You were worried about the hospital food, like it was going to be bad and stuff. *(She laughs.)* You were worried
POET	How are you doing?
ANNA	Itchy. How's your girlfriend?
POET	Good. Really good.... We broke up
ANNA	Oh
POET	Yeah, she got tired of me, she found me too—
ANNA	Poetic?
POET	Yeah. I've missed you
ANNA	Yeah, Kings in the Corner can be pretty addictive.
POET	Do you need a lift anywhere?
ANNA	Yes, definitely
POET	Where you going?
ANNA	Anywhere.
MADELYN	The Acceptance.
AUNT	How do you think she's doing?
MADELYN	I dunno. She's got lice again. I'm not doing so good though

Scratch

MADELYN's clutching a painting to her chest.

AUNT	I just don't know what to do for her
MADELYN	Do you think maybe I could go to the hospital and see her? I know she's only seeing family but I really want to say—
AUNT	You don't think Anna's on drugs, do you?
MADELYN	No.
AUNT	I guess you'd know, you guys are close, right?
MADELYN	Maybe I could see her just for a bit
AUNT	But addicts can be very sneaky
MADELYN	Give her a couple things, you know, say—
AUNT	What? Oh honey, I don't know. She's in a lot of pain right now.
MADELYN	You know Anna hasn't been to see her yet
AUNT	What? You mean she hasn't been to the—
ANNA	Hey guys. How do I look?
AUNT	You look great
MADELYN	Yeah. You going back to the hospital?
ANNA	Do you think I should wear the red shoes or the strappy shoes? I want to look great-great.
AUNT	You going to take a sweater? It's getting cold.
MADELYN	Yeah. You look great-great

AUNT	You ready to go, we'll give you a lift home, Madelyn, on the way to the hospital
MADELYN	Yeah, thanks
ANNA	Actually I'm not going yet; I'm going for dinner first.
AUNT	Dinner?
MADELYN	Dinner?
ANNA	Yeah. The poet is making me dinner. You can just take Madelyn home, don't worry about. I'll take a cab to the hospital.
AUNT	Oh, okay
MADELYN	Okay.

MADELYN sits around pages and pages of yellow portraits of the MOTHER. They cover her and the ground around her.

I'm moving out of my yellow period. My mom told me I had to give them space. Make myself available. But give them space? I told her it wasn't fair. She said, "Oh Madelyn." Then I started to cry. She said, "What do you want?" I thought, *you fundamentally don't get me, fundamentally!* I said, "I want chocolate." Then she went out and got me some chocolate. She bought me a lot of chocolate. I do love her. She's my mom. Yeah I'm done with yellow. I feel sick. I ate too much

FATHER	Hello
AUNT	How are you?
FATHER	Still standing, you?

AUNT   I sat next to her, I sat next to her and she held my hand; my sister's hand.

FATHER   I don't know what to say, I've run out of things to say.

AUNT   I sat beside her. I am so... I sat beside her—what time is it? Where's Anna, she said she was coming—she went for dinner with that poet guy who you hired this summer. She's taking a cab to the hospital—don't worry, *(laughs nervously)* I believe in cabs. I like being warm from one place to the next, waste of money but I believe in them. Do I need to worry about this guy, is something happening between them? Do you know him at all?

FATHER   No, but they say he's a specialist. I guess that's good. I guess it depends on what he's a specialist in though, right?

AUNT   No, the poet, should I worry about Anna and that poet spending so much time together?

FATHER   Oh. No. He's a nice guy. Terrible poet. Nice guy

AUNT   I don't know. Just the same, I'll have him over for hummus and some poker to assess the situation. Don't worry. This mysterious poet who cooks dinners will be checked out. A good old aunt inspection

FATHER   That's good

AUNT   Does she look thin too you, her pupils look okay?

FATHER   She looks like she's dying *(crying)*

AUNT   No. Not—

FATHER   I guess that's supposed to be how you look. I don't really notice it though, too much. Just sometimes I lose focus on the pillow, or the water, or the position of her neck, and I. I see what she looks like. For a second I see and then it's... *that's a dying woman*. And I'm looking at *a dying woman*. She's dying. My wife is dying *(he weeps)*

AUNT   I know. Hey? It's okay, you've been amazing with her, you have been amazing

FATHER   I hope so... I don't know what I am going to do, I love her so much

AUNT   I know.

        ANNA enters.

AUNT   Anna. You're here

FATHER   You came

MADELYN   The Goodbye.

MOTHER   It's hard to separate everything. It's hard. I don't see it all. I don't feel it all. There are moments, yes, where something makes sense, I think; a calm, the hum of something else, another possibility, but then other times, I'm scared, I am so scared, it is so uncomfortable to almost... to almost. It is so uncomfortable to be alive and... Anna?

        The MOTHER's arms outstretched.

        I didn't think you'd come. I thought it would be too hard. I thought— Oh Anna

ANNA   Of course I'm here. Look at this mess *(referring to the amount of clutter, cleaning and medical instruments)*

	Someone should—it's bright in here, eh, do you want me to—
MOTHER	You're my baby. My baby girl
ANNA	I know
MOTHER	You were in my arms. I held you all little and soft. You're my baby
ANNA	Mom, I know
MOTHER	Come here.
ANNA	You comfortable, do you need anything?
MOTHER	Just to kiss those cheeks
ANNA	Mom.

She offers up her cheeks.

MOTHER	Someday people are going to line up to kiss those cheeks
ANNA	Mom, seriously— I'm not going into the business of cheek-kissing. Mom? What's wrong—are you?
MOTHER	Nothing, I just have to sit up. I'm all twisted to the right. Makes me angry. I've always lived my life on the left side of things.

They both try to laugh.

ANNA	Do you want me to get someone? Dad, a doctor, one of those hot ones?
MOTHER	*(She laughs.)* No. No. I just gotta…. If you could just put a pillow behind this elbow, yeah that's great.

Okay, yes, here I am. Hello arms. Hello legs. Hello daughter... I want

ANNA   What, I'll get you whatever you need, water, more pillows, ice—

MOTHER   No, no—I want you to come closer, come closer to me.

ANNA does, she sits next to her MOTHER.

ANNA   I'm here, whatever you want I will do.

MOTHER   I want you to go to university.

ANNA   Totally

MOTHER   And get rid of the lice

ANNA   ...Mom?

MOTHER   I keep remembering the sensation of holding you in the water, your whole being in my arms, all of you, I had all of you. Oh, Anna, the way our skins felt next to each other, so soft, Anna, so soft. That sensation, your skin touching mine touching water, that's what seems important now. That feeling, that moment. That is my favourite moment. I'd live in that moment

ANNA   Mommy

MOTHER   I know.

Pause.

You're going to be okay.

ANNA   I can't—

MOTHER	I know you're going to be okay.
	She walks out dazed.
AUNT	How did it go? You okay? Oh baby
ANNA	I have to get rid of my lice. I have to—
FATHER	The doctor told me they'll be moving her home soon. Just for the final stages
ANNA	And I have to go to university
AUNT	What stage are we in now? It's okay, we'll figure it out
ANNA	She can't come home, I'm not ready
FATHER	They are going to set up palliative care. She'll be more comfortable in her own house. With her family around her
ANNA	I need to get rid of my lice
AUNT	I've called Licebusters
FATHER	It's going to be a lot more work. But she'll be happier, more peaceful.
AUNT	Yes, it will be better.
FATHER	It will be okay.
	They are all trying to lift the MOTHER and move her again, ANNA can't watch.
ANNA	I can't see my mom. I can't see this part. I can't see her till I'm rid of my lice.
FATHER	We'll just have to work out a system

AUNT	We'll set up a schedule, pain management. We're in the final stages. We're almost done. This part's almost over
FATHER	I'm doing well
AUNT	He is
FATHER	She's doing well too
AUNT	I am
ANNA	I can't do this.
FATHER	There is a way of existing when things are really bad that is almost easier than when things are normal. Because every step is… this is it… this is it. As opposed to just…
AUNT	This is, this is…

ANNA calms herself and walks to MADELYN.

ANNA	*(She takes a deep breath.)* I'm just so nervous, do you really just suck? Like what do you think the *blow* part means exactly?

MADELYN tries to clear all the pictures.

MADELYN	I don't know, why do you care?
ANNA	Older guys care about blow jobs. That is at least one thing I know for sure.

MADELYN makes a sound of disgust.

I just, I lack a sense of rhythm. I'm worried that's going to affect it. It's all about rhythm, isn't it?

MADELYN	I really don't know, it repulses me, Anna

ANNA	What are those? Are those my mother's paints?
MADELYN	Yes…. She gave them to me
ANNA	Those are her favourites, why would she give them to you?
MADELYN	This summer, she let me use them
ANNA	I should bring them back to her. She'll need them
MADELYN	No. They're—
ANNA	She'll need her paints back
MADELYN	Anna
ANNA	They're not yours
MADELYN	Let me give them to her then. I'll go and give them to her
ANNA	What's your problem? She needs them to paint. Just give them to me—

ANNA reaches for them.

MADELYN	No, I need them
ANNA	She needs them

They fight till they are pulling at each other's hair.

MADELYN	No
ANNA	Gimme them! She needs them. She needs them to paint!
MADELYN	She's never going to paint again, Anna!

ANNA   Excuse me?

MADELYN   I just—this is all I have. I'm sorry. I'm so sorry. I didn't mean to say—

ANNA   Fine. I'll take them later when you can detach from them emotionally or whatever

MADELYN   I didn't mean to say that she was...

ANNA   I'm going to go to my boyfriend's now, my poetic older boyfriend's, to be supported, to have dinner, and to try and give him a blow job.... She can just buy new paints, I guess, if she needs to.

    ANNA walks away.

MADELYN   *(itches her head)* Fuck. To be left.... I never got to go see her at the hospital. Or at the house. I waited. I waited for someone to ask me. Someone to say, "She's ready to see you now."/I waited to be by Anna's side and go hand in hand, face the world together, the hospital, the home, her mother.... But no one asked me.... That makes me so—this is her story and her feelings and.... If what you feel is more than appropriate, you have to bury it? I bury it in my pillow, in my hands and my—I bury it in all the colours around me, so the world is singing sadness, so all the blues and greens and yellows know my sadness, know me. It's just—I feel like I'm feeling more than her sometimes.... She.... She is.... She's always at her boyfriend's house, while her mother is.... No, it's not that I don't.... She must. It must. If this was my story, I would tell you why she meant a lot to me. I wanted a goodbye. I needed to say goodbye. But instead I bought a magazine and some more chocolate, and dozed in what doesn't matter. But it does matter, because, because, I'm completely alone. If this were my story, I'd tell it through my bed. Because it carries me and I am, I am so heavy in it. My brothers were really nice to me. For one day their footsteps were whispers and they talked to me like I was breakable. Shhh. I'm already broken. I have no rights because I'm not her and I can just—all I can do is just feel. And if this were my story you'd know how heavy that is.

ANNA   When your mother's dying you are allowed to just eat whatever you want.

The POET hands her a piece of cake.

You bake too?

POET   I bake.

ANNA   *(taking a bite of cake)* Anything you want. You're allowed. If there was a handbook it'd say that you're allowed. It would also say you could kiss whoever you wanted. You'd be allowed to kiss whoever.

POET   Anna, I...

ANNA   Yes?

POET   I want to share something with you. It's about your mother. I've been working on it since.... I wrote a poem.

ANNA   Oh.

POET   ...it's called "Perfect Pain... and the Potato"... *(clears his throat)* It was round and tough, fresh from the earth and rough. I wanted it to be everything, the final step. For weeks I tested it, I gave it every different taste. Part of love is memorizing, simple, and pure, learning someone fully, getting all their details right, like cooking slowly—letting the flavour fight. I waited till it was ready, perfect and done, the skin got so much softer, warmed from the inside out. I took it out and fed it to her, the final step, the last hurray. A perfect potato. Sometimes pain is beautiful and that, that is okay.

ANNA looks at him like he is a complete moron, confused and weirded out, she grabs him and kisses him.

I'm…. I can't… your—

ANNA   I am in so much pain.

POET goes and kisses her again softly.

Oh. Yes. I like that…

POET   Yes

ANNA   Can we use our tongues now?

They kiss. They kiss some more.

POET   This feels—

ANNA   Good. Better. Okay

POET   Yes.

You're beautiful

ANNA   Like her.

POET   Yeah.

ANNA unbuttons his pants. ANNA whispers.

ANNA   What do I do?

Scratch

POET	I—well, I'm not sure?
ANNA	Oh really?
POET	I mean… you just kind of suck. But, you don't have to do this, Anna.
ANNA	Can you show me?
POET	Ah—no, I can't exactly show you… Anna you don't—
ANNA	Okay, cool. Right, cool. You just kinda… yeah, cool, I'm all over it.

She begins to go down on him. He makes groaning noises.

POET	Oh. Oh yes. Oh. Oh. Oh
ANNA	I'm doing good?
POET	Oh. Yes, yes. Yes. Oh, oh, oh God!

The phone rings just as the POET orgasms.

ANNA turns to the audience, come in her hair, as the POET answers the phone.

Hello. Yes. Yes, she's here; I was just feeding her dinner, you know, taking care. Yeah, she's right here.

He hands her the phone.

ANNA	Hi… oh… okay. Right, I'll go. Yeah, yeah it's okay. I'll just take a cab. Yeah it's fine…. I have money…. Bye. *(She hangs up.)* Uh… I have to go now. My mother is dead
POET	Oh my God. She's…

77

ANNA	Yeah.
POET	You okay? I mean, of course you're not. I mean.... Here.

> *He hands her a tissue. She doesn't know what to do with it. It can't get the come out of her hair.*

ANNA	Yeah... I'm just going to call a cab, my aunt has this cab thing, she likes me to take cabs everywhere, we have like a jar for cab money, but I guess it makes sense now, I guess if there was ever a time to take a cab this would be it, I've got to go now, I've gotta call a cab, do you know a cab number? Yeah, I gotta go now, I can hail one, I can—
POET	Anna... I'm sorry...
ANNA	Yeah whatever, it'll just wash out, right?
POET	No, about your mother
ANNA	Oh.
POET	Do you need me to come with you?
ANNA	Oh. What? No. I don't need you to come. No, I think you should stay here
POET	Oh my God
ANNA	Yeah. Thank you for dinner
POET	I can't believe she's gone. Really gone.

> *FATHER and AUNT stand around the MOTHER.*

FATHER	Anna
AUNT	Oh, sweetheart. Come here.

ANNA	*(She scratches.)* Where's Madelyn?
AUNT	She's in a better place now
ANNA	Yeah, well, we're in a worse place. I should call Maddy
AUNT	What do you want to do, what can we do for you?
ANNA	I want to go for a strawberry milkshake with Madelyn, where is she? Did anyone call her?
FATHER	Oh God. This is it. Oh God…. It's just a body. She is just a body now.
AUNT	She looks peaceful. Fly away, my sweet sister, fly up up up up away
FATHER	She looks…. If there was ever a question of souls… she looks…

They all turn to ANNA expectantly, ANNA just stares at her MOTHER. A long pause. MADELYN goes to her.

MADELYN	Anna
ANNA	I don't know how to tell this part
MADELYN	I know
ANNA	Madelyn, I… I can't do this, I'm… she's gone. I don't know how to do this. I don't…. I don't understand this. This, this, I don't get it. I can't do this. Her face. Oh God, her face. It's…. Her eyes, her cheeks, her temples, I want— I need. It's not that I don't believe this is happening, I do, I just… I just can't do it. This isn't how it's supposed to go… I can't do this part, I can't tell this part, I don't understand this part.
MADELYN	Come here.

*They hug, their bare hair touching. After a long moment
ANNA starts scratching.*

Anna

ANNA	I'm so itchy! I'm so itchy, Madelyn. I'm so itchy.
MADELYN	It's okay. It's okay. Shhhh. It's okay
ANNA	No it's not. It's not okay. This is not okay. I've been trying. I have really, I've been trying but… they won't go away. I keep scratching and scratching and the more I scratch the itchier I get and the— I have lice. I'm sorry Mom. I am so sorry. I'm so, so sorry. I still have lice. So much lice. I can't get them off. I can't. I can't. I can't. My mother's dead and I still have lice. Fuck!
MADELYN	Shhh. Shhh…. Oh Anna. We'll get them out. I'm going to do it. I'm going to get these suckers out. I can do that. That is something I can do. I know I can. I know how to get rid of lice
ANNA	They'll never go away. I don't know why they won't go away! They're eating me. You should be allowed a lifetime to die. That's how long you need to say goodbye.

*MADELYN takes ANNA's head and calmly begins nit
picking it, hair by hair.*

POET	If this were my story, it would be about pain, about feeding off of other's pain. I would tell you the way I fell in love her, the way I fell in love with both of them
AUNT	If this were my story, it would be about being the only one speaking out loud, the only one keeping track, being the healthy one, carrying the weight of your own health. It would be about what happened after

FATHER   If this were my story, it would be about how I loved her. How I loved loving her. How I lived for loving her. It would be about how having a child makes you measure time differently

MOTHER   If this were my story, I would tell it all backwards, towards life, to our skin touching. I'd tell you how scared I was. I'd tell you about stretching one moment out, stretching it out so much that there is a life in a moment

> *MADELYN finishes nit picking and begins to braid ANNA's hair.*

ANNA   In my story, it doesn't end, it repeats again and again. This is my part, all itchy and scabbed over, ready to be picked at again and again. I remember her voice and I remember her smell and I remember the time and the taste, and when these parts take too much to remember, I scratch at them, I scratch and I scratch and I scratch—I will never see my mother's face again

> *Lights fade as MADELYN finishes braiding ANNA's wild hair into two single, neat braids.*

MADELYN   If this were my story, I would tell you there are just parts, parts of people, parts of feelings, parts of smell, parts of colour, and parts of truth. Parts coming together to be something.... This isn't my story, but I am a part of it. And this is the part where I get rid of Anna's lice. This is a good part. Look,

> *She touches ANNA's head.*

ANNA   All done.

> *The end.*

Charlotte Corbeil-Coleman is a graduate of the National Theatre School of Canada (2008) in the playwriting program. Her first play, *The End of Pretending*, was a winner of the 2002 SummerWorks Eye Audience Choice Award, and went on to do a run at the Regent Theatre in Picton, Ontario. She is currently developing a screenplay and working on a collection of short stories, *I've Slept in Every Room but the Kitchen…* Charlotte lives in Toronto and is a playwright-in-residence at Factory Theatre.